SNAPSHOTS IN HISTORY

THE LITTLE ROCK NINE

Struggle for Integration

by Stephanie Fitzgerald

Struggle for Integration

by Stephanie Fitzgerald

Content Adviser: Derek Shouba, Adjunct History Professor
and Assistant Provost, Roosevelt University

Reading Adviser: Katie Van Sluys, Ph.D.,
School of Education, DePaul University

COMPASS POINT BOOKS
MINNEAPOLIS, MINNESOTA

COMPASS POINT BOOKS

3109 West 50th Street, #115
Minneapolis, MN 55410

Visit Compass Point Books on the Internet at
www.compasspointbooks.com
or e-mail your request to
custserv@compasspointbooks.com

For Compass Point Books
Jennifer VanVoorst, Jaime Martens, XNR Productions, Inc.,
Catherine Neitge, Keith Griffin, and Carol Jones

Produced by White-Thomson Publishing Ltd.

For White-Thomson Publishing
Stephen White-Thomson, Susan Crean, Amy Sparks, Tinstar Design
Ltd., Derek Shouba, Justine Dunn, Laurel Haines, and Timothy Griffin

Library of Congress Cataloging-in-Publication Data
Fitzgerald, Stephanie.
  The Little Rock Nine : Struggle for Integration / Stephanie Fitzgerald.
     p. cm. — (Snapshots in history)
  Includes bibliographical references and index.

  ISBN-13: 0-7565-2011-3 (hardcover)
  ISBN-10: 0-7565-2011-8 (hardcover)

1. School integration—Arkansas—Little Rock—History—20th
century—Juvenile literature. 2. Central High School (Little Rock,
Ark.)—History—20th century—Juvenile literature. 3. African American
students—Education (Secondary)—Arkansas—Little Rock—History—
20th century—Juvenile literature. I. Title. II. Series.
  LC214.23.L56F57 2007
  373.767'73–dc22   2006004416

THE LITTLE ROCK NINE

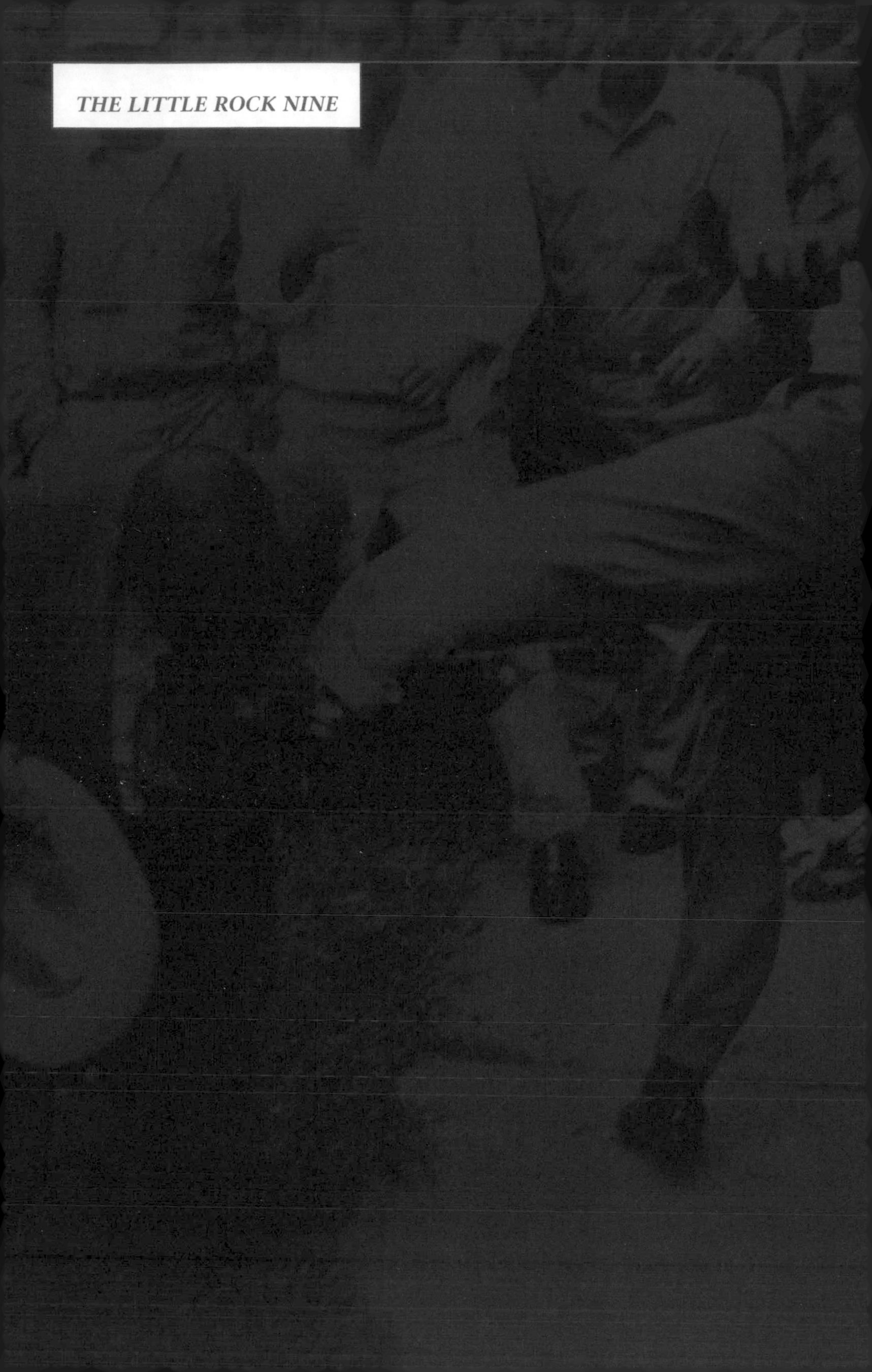

Contents

Alone in the Crowd

Chapter

1

On the morning of September 4, 1957, 15-year-old Elizabeth Eckford said a prayer and got ready for school. She was wearing a new dress that she had made for the occasion, because this was not any ordinary school day. Today, Elizabeth and nine other black students would be enrolling at Central High School in Little Rock, Arkansas. They would be the first black students ever to attend the school, and many white people did not want them there.

Elizabeth had been so nervous the night before that she could not sleep. Instead she read her Bible and found comfort in the words, "The Lord is my light and my salvation; whom shall I fear? the Lord is the strength of my life; of whom shall I be afraid?"

As she neared the school, Elizabeth tried not to be afraid even though she had much to fear. A crowd of angry white people had already gathered in front of the school. They were determined not to let in the 10 black pupils. Elizabeth did not see any of the other black students in front of the school. She was quite alone—and surrounded by a sea of angry white faces.

White students, like Hazel Bryant, shouted at Elizabeth Eckford as she walked toward Central High.

Elizabeth did not know that the other black students had made a plan the night before to meet in the morning and walk into the school together. They had not been able to talk to Elizabeth because her family did not own a telephone.

Suddenly, Elizabeth heard someone in the crowd yell out:

TWO OPPOSING SIDES

There were two opposing sides to the struggle to integrate schools in the United States. Segregationists wanted black and white students to each have their own schools—as well as other public places such as restaurants, theaters, and restrooms. Integrationists believed that black and white people should be able to share schools and other public places.

Here she comes, get ready!

As if this had been their cue, everyone else in the mob started to shout insults at the teenager. Later in the day, Elizabeth explained how she felt at that moment:

My knees started to shake all of a sudden, and I wondered whether I could make it to the center entrance a block away. It was the longest block I ever walked in my whole life.

From where she stood, Elizabeth could see members of the Arkansas National Guard standing at the school entrance. She thought they were there to make sure that she and the nine other black students made it safely into the school. But when she got closer, a soldier blocked the entrance and waved her away. Elizabeth turned to another soldier. He did not speak to her. He and the other soldiers who joined him just raised their bayonet-tipped rifles and blocked her path. It was clear that Elizabeth was not going to be allowed into the school. She had no choice but to turn around and walk back through the angry mob that filled the street.

Elizabeth held her head high, pretending she could not hear the nasty remarks that were being shouted at her. As she walked through the crowd, peopled yelled:

Lynch her! Lynch her!

The people in the crowd were not just talking about hitting Elizabeth, or even knocking her down to the ground. They were talking about actually killing her—a 15-year-old schoolgirl—simply because she was trying to attend an all-white school.

Her eyes hidden behind dark sunglasses, Elizabeth scanned the white faces in the crowd, hoping to find someone who might help her. She spotted an old lady who she thought had a kind face. But as Elizabeth turned her head, the woman spit on her.

LYNCHING

Lynching refers to when a mob, or angry group of people, attack and kill another person—most commonly by hanging. Between 1882 and 1968, there were almost 4,000 reported lynchings of black people in the United States. Though the mob usually accused the victim of some offense or crime—anything from murder to simply ignoring the unwritten rules of how to behave in segregated society—there was rarely an official investigation or trial, and the killers were rarely punished for their crimes.

The streets were filled with students, protesters, and reporters on what should have been the first day of school for Elizabeth.

Elizabeth kept walking. Nearly 500 angry adults surrounded her and walked along with her, calling her ugly names. Elizabeth fought to control her tears as news photographers took pictures. Elizabeth spotted a bus stop in the distance. She felt that if she could just make it to that bench, she would be safe. As she soon found out, it was not the bus stop that would save her.

Elizabeth sat down on the bench with her head bowed as people continued to jeer. One person even suggested to the crowd:

Get a rope and drag her over to this tree.

Benjamin Fine, an education reporter, was covering the story for *The New York Times*. He sat down next to Elizabeth, put his arm around her, and whispered:

Don't let them see you cry.

At the same time, a white woman named Grace Lorch struggled through the mob toward Elizabeth. She was furious, screaming at the crowd:

Leave this child alone! Why are you tormenting her? Six months from now, you will hang your heads in shame.

Lorch moved to the other side of Elizabeth to offer her comfort and protection, while she put the mob on alert:

I'm just waiting for one of you to dare touch me! I'm just aching to punch somebody in the nose!

The crowd was enraged that two white people would take the side of a black girl. They turned their hatred on Lorch and Fine and started calling them horrible names.

13

When the bus finally came, Lorch helped Elizabeth on board and watched as it pulled away. Elizabeth took the bus to the Negro School for the Deaf and Blind, where her mother worked in the laundry room. Elizabeth ran to find her mother, with whom she could finally find comfort.

Elizabeth did not realize that news of what had happened at the school had been spreading through the town. False reports that Elizabeth had been physically injured when she tried to enter school had reached her parents. Elizabeth's father left work to search for her. Her mother waited and prayed.

When Elizabeth found her mother, she was standing at a window with her head bowed. As Elizabeth entered the room, her mother turned—it was clear she had been crying. Elizabeth later recalled:

> *I wanted to tell her I was all right. But I couldn't speak. She put her arms around me and I cried.*

Newspapers across the country covered the scene at Central High School. The word spread very quickly about how Elizabeth—and the other black students who had tried to enter the school at another door—had been treated that day. Pictures of white people yelling at the teenagers were splashed across newspapers. Many people— both black and white—were shocked at how the children had been treated. They could not imagine how the students could bear to try to enter Central High School again. In fact, one of the 10 would never return to Central at all. The other nine would not return right away.

A story in a local Arkansas newspaper showed the black students being turned away by National Guardsmen.

The group that came to be known as the Little Rock Nine refused to give up. They knew the importance of their mission. They understood that by standing up to hatred and racism, by challenging the system of segregation, they were changing the world for the better. As soon as the Little Rock Nine agreed to try to integrate Central High School, they knew how difficult their lives would become. But they refused to be bullied or scared away.

By quietly and courageously standing up for their rights, the Little Rock Nine made progress for all Americans. They helped change the education system in America and brought worldwide attention to their inspiring example. ◗

Eight of the students met with the U.S. Attorney and the FBI to answer questions about being turned away from Central High School. Pictured from left: Carlotta Walls, Gloria Ray, Ernest Green, Jefferson Thomas, Thelma Mothershed, Terrence Roberts, Minnijean Brown, and Jane Hill.

17

With All Deliberate Speed

Chapter 2

By 1957, African-Americans had been fighting for equal rights for generations. From the time that they were first brought to this country as slaves, black people were treated as less than human. Even after slavery was abolished, Jim Crow laws were put into place, especially in the South. These laws kept black people and white people separated. Black people were not permitted in many restaurants and hotels, and where they were permitted, they had separate— and inferior—public facilities, like restrooms, drinking fountains, and waiting rooms. Many white people treated black people with disrespect and were often cruel.

By the late 1950s, many white people falsely believed that blacks and whites were living together without any problems. However, at that time, many ordinary black people were afraid to speak out against their unfair conditions. Black people who complained about poor treatment could be harassed or fired from their jobs. At worst, they could be killed.

In the segregated South, African-Americans had to use separate waiting rooms at bus stations.

Not all white people were violently racist, of course. Some were just used to living with the situation as it was—they grew up with the notion that black people had a separate place in society and saw no reason why that should change. Others actively tried to improve the situation by working with civil rights organizations. White activists were in the minority, especially in the South. However, there were black civil rights organizations—and individual activists—fighting for equal rights every day.

CIVIL RIGHTS ORGANIZATIONS

The National Association for the Advancement of Colored People (NAACP), which was formed in 1909, is just one organization dedicated to improving the rights of African-Americans. Among other things, this organization uses the court system to fight and change unfair laws. Other civil rights organizations, such as the Southern Christian Leadership Conference (SCLC), used protests and boycotts to bring about change.

Little by little, these people were making progress: Buses, lunch counters, and waiting rooms had become integrated, and more jobs were becoming available to African-Americans—even in the South. But the education system was lagging far behind. Many schools were still segregated, and black schools usually had inferior equipment and hand-me-down books.

Changing conditions soon became the focus of civil rights activists. They knew that a quality education would help African-Americans get better jobs and gain more power. They felt that integration of schools was needed in order for black students to have the same opportunities as white students.

Thanks to the efforts of civil rights activists, the U.S. Supreme Court outlawed segregation in public schools on May 17, 1954, in the landmark *Brown v. Board of Education* case. Unfortunately, the court softened its decision a year later by ruling that the order should be implemented not immediately, but "with all deliberate speed." This vague wording meant that local governments and judges could delay progress for years.

All over the country, African-Americans marched to protest segregation.

Most school districts in the South took the phrase "all deliberate speed" to mean as slowly as possible. From 1954 to 1964, less than 1 percent of black children attended "white" schools in the South. In fact, a number of Southern legislatures passed laws that penalized school districts that attempted to integrate.

In 1954, Little Rock, Arkansas, was a city in which segregation was the norm. Black people and white people had little to do with each other socially, and each attended their own schools. However, the Little Rock School Board accepted the Supreme Court's decision and began working on a plan for integration. Their interpretation of "all deliberate speed" meant that the Little Rock plan would not get under way for three years.

SECOND-CLASS SCHOOLS

There was a big difference in the quality of black and white schools in Little Rock. By about 1940, the city was spending $67 per year on each white student, but only $40 per year on each black student. That meant that black schools did not have up-to-date textbooks, enough playground space, or adequate equipment for science classes and extracurricular clubs.

The Blossom Plan, which was named after Little Rock School Superintendent Virgil Blossom, called for gradual integration in three phases. During the 1957–1958 school year, the senior high schools (grades 10–12) would be integrated. Once that was successful, the junior high schools (grades 7–9) would follow. And then, finally, the elementary schools (grades 1–6) would be integrated.

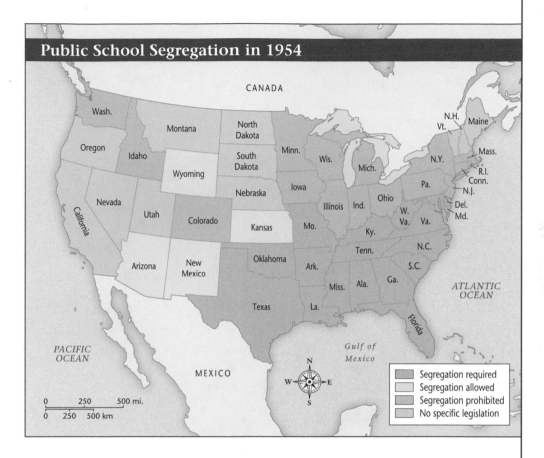

Public School Segregation in 1954

CANADA

Wash.

Montana

North Dakota

Oregon

Idaho

Wyoming

South Dakota

Minn.

Wis.

Mich.

N.H.

Vt.

Maine

Mass.

N.Y.

R.I.

Conn.

Nebraska

Iowa

Pa.

N.J.

Nevada

Utah

Colorado

Kansas

Illinois

Ind.

Ohio

W. Va.

Va.

Del.

Md.

California

Mo.

Ky.

Arizona

New Mexico

Oklahoma

Ark.

Tenn.

N.C.

S.C.

Miss.

Ala.

Ga.

ATLANTIC OCEAN

Texas

La.

Florida

PACIFIC OCEAN

Gulf of Mexico

MEXICO

N

W E

S

0   250   500 mi.
0 250 500 km

Segregation required
Segregation allowed
Segregation prohibited
No specific legislation

Many civil rights activists thought this plan was too slow—after all, it would not even start for three years. Daisy Lee Gatson Bates, for one, was disgusted with the plan. Bates ran a black newspaper with her husband that often exposed the injustices in Southern society. She was also the president of the Arkansas chapter of the National Association for the Advancement of Colored People (NAACP). Bates talked to the NAACP's national leaders and came up with a plan of her own. In the winter of 1955–1956, she helped organize 33 black students who wanted to attend white schools in Little Rock.

Most schools in the South were not integrated until after 1964.

23

When Bates attempted to enroll the children, however, the principals of all the schools refused to let them in. They said that the families would have to take it up with Superintendent Blossom. Bates narrowed her list of students down to

Daisy Bates and Arkansas NAACP Officer Clarence Laws worked for integration.

nine—one for each grade—before presenting it to the superintendent. He, too, refused to enroll the students in the white schools.

On February 8, 1956, Wiley Branton, a lawyer for the NAACP, filed a suit in federal court. He claimed that the Little Rock School Board was discriminating against the black students by keeping them out of the schools. At the trial in August later that year, a federal judge ruled that the school board was acting with "reasonable speed" by adopting the Blossom plan. NAACP lawyers, including Thurgood Marshall, decided to appeal the case. Marshall was a civil rights lawyer who later became the first African-American to sit on the highest court in the country—the Supreme Court. In March 1957, the U.S. Court of Appeals ruled that Little Rock had to begin integration that year. Although the ruling did not speed up integration, it did guarantee that the Blossom Plan would have to start as planned that year.

GREAT CRUSADER

When she was only a child, Daisy Lee Gatson Bates learned firsthand what it meant to be black in America. Bates' mother was killed by white men, and her father had to escape so he, too, would not be killed. The murderers were never charged or punished for their crime. The cruelty of this act and the unfairness of it all caused Bates to hate white people for a while. When she was in her 20s, the words of Bates' adoptive father caused her to refocus her feelings. He said:

You're filled with hatred. Hate can destroy you, Daisy. Don't hate white people just because they're white. Hate the humiliations we live under in the South. Hate the discrimination that eats away at every black man and woman. Hate the insults. And then try to do something about it.

Bates dedicated the rest of her life to the civil rights movement.

25

Once the decision was made to integrate Little Rock's Central High School, opposition came from all sides. Segregationists did not want white and black children going to school together—and they were prepared to commit violence to keep it from happening.

Two local groups that took the lead in opposing integration were the Capital Citizens' Council and the Mothers' League of Central High School. Other segregationists came from other parts of the state—even from different states—to protest at Central. No one was sure at first, though, which side the Arkansas governor was on.

By 1957, Arkansas Governor Orval E. Faubus was in his second term. He had a good record on racial issues. He had overseen the appointment of a number of African-Americans to state office, and his state had desegregated more schools than 11 other Southern states combined. In fact, some of his opponents even accused him of sympathizing with—or belonging to—the NAACP. Based on his record, integrationists were hoping that even if he did not completely support school integration he would not try to stop it. On August 29, 1957, Faubus' position was revealed.

Two days earlier, Mrs. Clyde A. Thomason, the Mothers' League recording secretary, filed a suit to try to prevent the integration of Central High School. When she testified at the August 29 hearing, Thomason said that there would be violence if

Central opened as an integrated school. She said that rumors were going around about two gangs— one that was white, the other black—who were buying knives and guns.

Governor Faubus held a press conference at the Arkansas State Capitol.

Another witness, Police Chief Marvin Potts, testified that there was no reason to believe that violent gangs would cause trouble at the school opening. Both Superintendent Blossom and the president of the Little Rock School Board agreed— neither expected any problems at the school. The testimony of three such reliable witnesses should have ended the case right there. But then a surprise witness took the stand.

Governor Faubus testified that he personally knew of cases in which guns had been taken from black and white students. He said that he did not think the citizens of Little Rock would let integration occur peacefully.

Apparently, Governor Faubus had decided to do what would make him politically popular, rather than what he knew was the right thing to do. At that time, white people made up about 78 percent of the population of Arkansas—and most of them were against integration. Faubus wanted to win a third term as governor when elections occurred the next year, and he knew that supporting integration might cost him that election.

Mostly because of the governor's testimony, the judge ruled in favor of Thomason. Integration of the school was put on hold. By this time, 10 promising young black students had been selected to integrate Central High School. Now they did not know where—or even if—they would be starting their school year.

Three days after the ruling, Wiley Branton and Thurgood Marshall went before the U.S. District Court asking to have the order overruled. The U.S. District Court is a regional court that hears cases that have to do with federal law. The integrationists won their appeal. Judge Ronald Davies ruled that the integration must proceed as planned. He also issued an order that no one was allowed to interfere with the black students as they entered the school.

By 9 P.M. on September 2, the day before school was to start, 300 Arkansas National Guardsmen began to surround Central High School. Governor Faubus had called the emergency troops to active duty. He claimed they were not there to help or hinder the integration, only to "keep the peace." But when he spoke on radio and television at 10:15 that evening, he made his position very clear:

CALL OUT THE GUARD

In 1903, state militias were organized into the National Guard system. Each state has its own National Guard, which is made up of troops that are controlled by that state's government and equipped by the federal government.

It is my opinion that it will not be possible to restore or to maintain order and protect the lives and property of the citizens if forcible integration is carried out tomorrow. The schools, for the time being, must be operated on the same basis as they have in the past.

29

A SPLASH OF COLOR

Even though no black children tried to attend Central High School on the first day of school, 400 white people showed up to protest integration. In fact, the only black person on the campus that day was a reporter named L.C. Bates, who had come to cover the event for his newspaper. When white newsmen asked what he was doing there, Bates replied, "I just came by to add some color to the occasion."

Hundreds of people gathered in front of Little Rock's Central High School on September 3 to protest integration.

On September 3, a total of 2,000 students entered the school. None of them was black. The presence of the National Guard had put the integrationists' plans on hold. Superintendent Blossom and the school board turned to Judge Davies for advice—should they go forward with integration? Davies said that they should assume that the troops were not there to stop integration, but only to keep the peace. He recommended that the black students plan to attend school the next day. 🔖

31

The Little Rock Nine

Chapter

3

When the decision to integrate Central High School was first made, Superintendent Blossom asked the principals of the city's black junior and senior high schools to give him a list of pupils who were interested in attending Central. Ultimately, the superintendent and the school board would select a number of children from that list to integrate Central High School.

Many children jumped at the chance to be the first black students to attend the all-white high school. Central High School was a big, beautiful school that took up two whole city blocks. It had five floors of classrooms, marble staircases, and a fountain in the entrance. More importantly, it had all the latest lab equipment and brand-new textbooks.

The students realized that a diploma from Central High School would give them a better start in life than one from Horace Mann, Little Rock's black high school.

Before integration, African-Americans were forbidden to attend Central High School in Little Rock.

There was a lot riding on the integration of Central High School, so the principals knew they had to choose students carefully. The students selected had to be hardworking and have very good grades. They also had to have the right type of personality to survive in an all-white school—especially one where they were not particularly welcome.

Adults in the black community knew that the students selected for integration would be tested again and again. They would be insulted, threatened, and perhaps even physically harmed. This was not a task that just anyone could undertake.

Eventually, the principals gave Superintendent Blossom a list of about 80 students who said they wanted the chance to attend Central. The school board had no intention of introducing 80 black children to a school of 2,000 students, though. Blossom told the principals to pare down the list. He told them to remove the names of the students who might not be "mentally and emotionally equipped" to integrate the school. The principals then came back with a list of 32 black pupils.

Blossom met with the remaining 32 students and their families individually. He stressed to them how difficult it would be to integrate an all-white school. In fact, some people believe he tried to scare some of the students away on purpose. Whatever really happened in those meetings, 15 students

Jackie Robinson broke baseball's color barrier when he joined the Brooklyn Dodgers in April 1947. Though he faced great opposition — including threats to his life and the lives of his family — Robinson never let racism get the better of him.

JUST LIKE JACKIE

Superintendent Blossom knew that the black students would be challenged by white students at Central. He told NAACP leaders that the kids should model their behavior after Jackie Robinson, the first black baseball player in the major leagues. Robinson responded to racial slurs and threats by ignoring them. To help them prepare to attend Central, a minister from Nashville, Tennessee, gave the students lessons in nonviolent resistance.

decided then and there that Central was not really right for them. Before school started in September, seven additional pupils changed their minds about attending Central.

35

The 10 students who were finally selected to integrate Central High School were 12th grader Ernest Green, 11th graders Terrence Roberts, Elizabeth Eckford, Minnijean Brown, Thelma Mothershed, Gloria Ray, and Melba Pattillo, and 10th graders Jefferson Thomas, Carlotta Walls, and Jane Hill. The reason this group came to be known as the "Little Rock Nine" and not the "Little Rock Ten" is because Jane Hill chose to attend Horace Mann. She made that decision after her first attempt to attend Central on September 4.

Ernest Green was someone the other eight kids could look up to—not only because he was the eldest, but also because he had an inner strength and a great sense of humor. Ernest had worked as a locker room attendant at a country club in Little Rock and had already met some of the white kids from Central, so he thought he would not have any problem fitting in. More importantly, Ernest knew even then the importance of his role as an integration pioneer. As an adult, he said:

> *We wanted to widen options for ourselves and later for our children.*

Terrence Roberts was a smart, talkative junior with a wild sense of humor. He loved to cheer up the other black pupils with impressions of the students and officials at Central. Terrence

Ernest Green

Terrence Roberts

Elizabeth Eckford

Minnijean Brown

had a lot of friends at his old school and thought that he could win over even the most racist white kids just by the force of his personality.

It is interesting that Elizabeth Eckford has become the most recognized of the Little Rock Nine because she was caught alone on her first day of school. Elizabeth was really a very quiet, serious girl. Elizabeth was strong willed and had what has been called a regal bearing, which is a way to say she had a sense of quiet dignity. Elizabeth never would have intentionally put herself at the front of the publicity surrounding the integration of Central High School.

Minnijean Brown was a tall and attractive 16-year-old. Minnijean was a great singer who was brimming with self-confidence. She was optimistic, and she just knew she would get along great with her new classmates. Unfortunately, Minnijean's upbeat attitude and positive self-image would soon make her a favorite target of the segregationist students in school.

37

Thelma Mothershed was a small, frail girl. She had a serious heart condition that caused her to lose her breath and sometimes feel faint. For this reason, her parents tried to talk her out of enrolling at Central. They thought the strain— both the physical and emotional strain— would be too much for their daughter. But Thelma refused to be talked out of going to the white school. Attending Central was much too important to her. Thelma wanted to become a teacher, and she knew that a diploma from Central would give her the opportunity to attend the best colleges. Neither she nor her family told Superintendent Blossom about her condition. Although he was always worried about her health, Thelma's father later admitted:

> *I was secretly pulling for her, and I was proud when she stood up to us.*

It is clear to see why Gloria Ray, who was also 15, was selected to transfer to Central High School. This charming girl was very serious about her studies. She was also careful about how she presented herself: She was always neat and beautifully dressed.

Melba Pattillo was only 12 years old when the landmark *Brown v. Board of Education* decision was made in 1954. Three years later, when her teacher asked for volunteers to integrate Central, Melba quickly raised her hand.

She later recalled:

> *As I signed my name on the paper they passed around, I thought about all those times I'd gone past Central High wanting to see inside. I was certain it would take a miracle to integrate Little Rock's schools. But I reasoned that if schools were open to my people, I would also get access to other opportunities I had been denied, like going to shows at Robinson Auditorium, or sitting on the first floor of the movie theater.*

Melba did not tell her family what she had done. When her parents found out that she had volunteered, they were very angry. They worried that their family would be attacked or that they might lose their jobs. But as soon as they realized that Melba was committed to integration, her grandmother, mother, and brother became her greatest sources of strength and support.

Sophomore Jefferson Thomas was athletic and had been a track star at his junior high school. As happened with Minnijean, though, the qualities that made him a success at his former school made segregationists single him out for abuse at Central.

NOTHING EXTRA

Many of the Little Rock Nine were very active in extracurricular activities at their old schools. Jefferson was on the track team and was a member of the student government at Dunbar Junior High School. Carlotta was a member of her school's student council. Minnijean was a singer and acted in many school plays. Before they started at Central High School, though, the black students were told that they would not be able to participate in any extracurricular activities. The segregationist students and parents did not want to share their clubs, teams, and theater groups with the black students.

39

Like Ernest Green, Carlotta Walls did not expect trouble from white students at Central. She was a very athletic, upbeat girl who lived in an integrated neighborhood. She played baseball with her black and white neighbors regularly, so she did not think she had anything to fear from the white students.

Many older members of the black community, however, were afraid for the students. They remembered all too well what happened to black people who made certain whites angry: Crosses were burned on their lawns, bomb threats were made to their homes, and sometimes they were killed. People were afraid that the Little Rock Nine would stir up trouble by attempting to integrate Central. They thought that all black people—not just integrationists—would suffer severe consequences. Melba remembered being approached by a woman at church who began to lecture her:

> *For a moment I feared she was going to haul off and hit me. She was beside herself with anger. I could barely get my good morning in because she was talking very loud, attracting attention as she told me I was too fancy for my britches and that other people in our community would pay for my uppity need to be with white folks.*

Despite the opposition, the students were determined to integrate Central High School.

Thelma Mothershed

Gloria Ray

Melba Pattillo

Jefferson Thomas

Carlotta Walls

After missing the first official day of school—September 3—the students were confused about what would happen next. They had been meeting with Daisy Bates and leaders of the NAACP all summer long in preparation for their new school and the new school year. They knew what was expected of them and how they should behave at Central High School. They had even imagined there would be protests that would surround their entrance to the school.

That evening, it was decided that the black students would start school the next day, September 4. Knowing that protesters had been at the school the previous day made Daisy Bates worry for the students' safety. She called the Reverend Dunbar Ogden Jr., a white minister who supported integration, and the two worked together to come up with a plan. They agreed that they and the students would meet a few blocks from the school at 8:30 the next morning. Ogden would bring as many ministers as he could get to join them as escorts.

Elizabeth Eckford was told to leave Central High School by National Guardsmen on September 4, 1957.

Ogden called other ministers and asked them to help escort the children to school, but none wanted to help. The black ministers said that Superintendent Blossom had told them to stay away. Blossom was worried that their presence might make bigoted protesters angry. Many white ministers gave other excuses.

Finally, Ogden came up with four people who were willing to help: Ogden's son David; another white minister, the Reverend Will Campbell; and two black ministers, the Reverend ZZ Driver and the Reverend Harry Bass.

Bates also asked the Little Rock police to send a car to the meeting place to protect the new black students. They promised to escort the students all the way to the school. By this time it was 3 A.M., but Bates still had to call all of the students to tell them about the meeting.

One by one, Bates got her message to the children. The only one she could not reach was Elizabeth Eckford, whose family did not have a phone. Bates thought about going to the railroad station where Elizabeth's father worked, but by this time it was very late and she was exhausted. She decided that she would have to get in touch with Elizabeth in the morning before she left for school.

The next day, as she drove to the meeting place, Bates heard a report of a girl who was being mobbed at the school. It was at that moment that she realized she had forgotten to get in touch with Elizabeth, who was on her own as she was turned away from Central. ◣

Turned Away

On the morning of September 4, 1957, eight of the 10 black students, Ernest, Minnijean, Terrence, Thelma, Gloria, Jefferson, Carlotta, and Jane, gathered at the meeting point. Elizabeth was heading to school on her own. As Melba and her mother were on their way to meet the others, they ran into trouble.

Melba and her mother parked a few blocks from the meeting place and started to walk toward the school when they heard a commotion. From where they stood, they could see Elizabeth. They recognized she was in trouble, but there was no way they could get to her. They were surrounded by an angry mob themselves. They tried to sneak away, but it was too late. A white man noticed them and yelled, "They're getting away!" Four men chased Melba and her mother.

More angry men, one of whom had a rope in his hand, quickly joined them. As they were racing toward their car, Melba's mother thrust the car keys into her daughter's hand. She told Melba that no matter what happened, she needed to get to the car and get away. Melba was horrified. There was no way she would leave her mother behind. But her mother's pace was slowing. One of the men behind her mother got close enough to grab her blouse; the fabric ripped and the man fell to the ground. Another man swung a branch at Melba's head, but he missed. The girl felt an icy fear: If the man had knocked her down, she would have been at the mercy of the mob. She could have been killed.

Finally, Melba reached the car. She started the engine and threw the passenger door open for her mother. As soon as her mother was inside, Melba gunned the engine and backed down the street as fast as she could. One of the men caught up to the car and started pounding on it. Another threw a brick at the windshield. But Melba did not slow down. Afraid to go home in case they were followed, Melba drove in circles for a while. Her mother did not let her stop to switch places—even though Melba did not have a license and had never done more than practice driving in a parking lot. There was too much at stake.

Meanwhile, the other eight students and their five escorts made their way through the angry crowd, trying to ignore the threats and nasty names.

As had happened to Elizabeth, the National Guard turned them away when they finally reached the entrance to the school. Lieutenant Colonel Marion Johnson told one of the escorts that the soldiers were acting under orders from Governor Faubus to keep the black students out of Central.

The eight students and their escorts left the campus and headed over to Superintendent Blossom's office. There was no reason why the National Guard should have kept the children out of school—and Daisy Bates wanted answers. They even went to the U.S. Attorney's office and to meet with the FBI. The children had to answer a lot of questions, but no one had any idea when—or even if—the children would get another chance to enroll at Central.

The students could not understand why they were being turned away from the school.

That night, Melba wrote in her diary:

> *I was disappointed not to see what is inside Central High School. I don't understand why the governor sent grown-up soldiers to keep us out. I don't know if I should go back. But Grandma is right, if I don't go back, they will think they have won. They will think they can use soldiers to frighten us, and we'll always have to obey them. They'll always be in charge if I don't go back to Central and make the integration happen.*

Not all the children would be able to bounce back from the horrifying experience, though. What happened that day was enough to convince Jane Hill to go to Horace Mann.

The children's meetings with the U.S. Attorney and the FBI set in motion an investigation—and involved the president of the United States. By ordering the National Guard to keep the children out, Governor Faubus had gone against a federal order. President Dwight D. Eisenhower was furious. A three-week period of negotiation started between the president and the governor, which was marked by telegrams, meetings, and—finally—threats.

STATE RELATIONS

Some segregationists said they were against integration because the federal government was interfering in what they felt was a states' rights issue, or something the state should decide. Historically, most issues related to race and segregation had been within each state's power to decide. Before slavery was abolished, for example, an individual state chose whether to be a slave state or a free state. A lot of people in Arkansas did not like the idea of the federal government forcing the state to accept integration.

47

Lieutenant Colonel Marion Johnson of the National Guard explained to Carlotta Walls (left), Jane Hill, Gloria Ray, and Ernest Green that they would not be allowed in school.

Later in the afternoon of September 4, 1957, Judge Davies of the District Court ordered an investigation to find out who was responsible for interfering with the court order to start integration. Three days later, the school board sent a petition to the court asking them to put a hold on integration so things could "cool down." It was denied by Judge Davies. That same day, President Eisenhower used very strong language to show his support of the Supreme Court's decision. He wrote:

> *When I became President I took an oath to support and defend the Constitution of the United States. The only assurance I can*

> *give you is that the Federal Constitution*
> *will be upheld by me by every legal means at*
> *my command.*

Governor Faubus had to know from that message that he was in for a fight—one that he could not win. Eisenhower made his position—and his power—very clear.

On September 10, Governor Faubus was served with a Federal Court summons. He was to appear at a hearing on September 20. Meanwhile, the National Guard remained posted around the school. Later that day, the Little Rock Nine announced that they would not try to enter the school again until after the hearing. According to Minnijean's mother, the children were disappointed, to say the least:

> *They were very excited before registration.*
> *They were so sure this thing was all taken care*
> *of and thought they would be accepted.*

The nine students were also worried about falling behind in their schoolwork. They could not go to Central while the National Guard was ordered to keep them out. They also could not return to their old schools, for that would be admitting defeat. Those opposed to integration would see that as a way to stop the process completely. To keep up, the children met to study together every day while they waited to return to school.

They were also tutored by professors at Philander Smith College, an African-American school in Little Rock. This time together gave the nine students a chance to build close relationships that would last a lifetime. These friendships—the only school friends they would have for a year—also gave each student the strength to go through with the ordeal of integration.

On September 20, Judge Davies ruled that Governor Faubus could not use the National Guard to keep the nine black students out of Central High School. The governor made an announcement that he would obey that order. He removed the National Guard and replaced them with Little Rock

President Eisenhower sent a telegram to Governor Faubus to express his support of the Supreme Court's decision to start integration.

IMMEDIATE RELEASE   September 5, 1957

James C. Hagerty, Press Secretary to the President

THE WHITE HOUSE

U. S. Naval Base
Newport, Rhode Island

THE PRESIDENT TODAY SENT THE
FOLLOWING TELEGRAM TO THE
HONORABLE ORVAL E. FAUBUS,
THE GOVERNOR OF ARKANSAS

The Honorable Orval E. Faubus
Governor of Arkansas
Little Rock, Arkansas

Your telegram received requesting my assurance of understanding
of and cooperation in the course of action you have taken on school
integration recommended by the Little Rock School Board and
ordered by the United States District Court pursuant to the mandate
of the United States Supreme Court.

When I became President, I took an oath to support and defend the
Constitution of the United States. The only assurance I can give
you is that the Federal Constitution will be upheld by me by every
legal means at my command.

There is no basis of fact to the statements you make in your telegram
that Federal authorities have been considering taking you into custody
or that telephone lines to your Executive Mansion have been tapped
by any agency of the Federal Government.

At the request of Judge Davies, the Department of Justice is
presently collecting facts as to interference with or failure to
comply with the District Court's order. You and other state
officials -- as well as the National Guard which, of course, is
uniformed, armed and partially sustained by the Government --
will, I am sure, give full cooperation to the United States District
Court.

Dwight D. Eisenhower

police officers. However, he said that he hoped the black students would choose to stay away from the school until everyone could be sure that integration could happen without any violence.

The Little Rock Nine studied together as they waited for permission to enter Central High School.

Once the students received the news that the National Guard was being removed, they prepared to start school the following Monday, September 23. Unfortunately, the presence of the police officers offered the students little security. Many of the men on the force were segregationists and did little to protect the students from protesters and other students.

51

Class Dismissed

Chapter

5

On the morning of Monday, September 23, 1957, the Little Rock Nine met at Daisy Bates' house so they could go to school together. They were frightened, but they were determined to get inside the school.

Meanwhile, a mob of 1,000 angry people had gathered outside the school. The students, who had piled into two cars, were met by the police and escorted into the school through a side entrance. At the time, they did not know how they had managed to avoid being seen by the crowd. As it turns out, four black newspaper reporters had arrived on the scene just five minutes before the students were sneaked into the school. As soon as the mob noticed the reporters, part of the crowd attacked them. Men in the mob kicked and punched *Arkansas State*

Press photographer Earl Davy and New York's *Amsterdam News* managing editor James Hicks, but it was *Memphis Tri-State Defender* reporter Alex Wilson who took the brunt of their abuse.

For their second attempt at enrollment, the black students were taken in to Central High through a side entrance.

14

Reporter Alex Wilson was brutally beaten by white protesters.

Several white men jumped on Wilson, threw him to the ground, and started kicking and punching him. As Wilson got up, one of his attackers yelled, "Run, nigger!" But Wilson, who had served as a U.S. Marine in World War II, refused to give them the satisfaction. Later, he explained why he would not run away:

> *The vision of Elizabeth Eckford ... flashed before me as she with dignity strode through a jeering, hooting [crowd] of segregationists several days ago.*

The fact that they could not intimidate Alex Wilson made his attackers even angrier. One of them even hit the reporter in the head with a brick. Very quickly, though, the mob's attention was turned again. Someone noticed that the black students had made it into the school.

DEADLY CONSEQUENCES

After the attack at Central High School, Alex Wilson suffered from headaches. He was later diagnosed with Parkinson's disease and died three years after the attack. Wilson's wife is sure that the blow to his head caused the illness that took her husband's life.

A shout went up alerting the other protesters, who went into a frenzy when they heard the news. Mothers yelled to their children to leave the school rather than stay inside with the black pupils. Others started chanting, "Two, four, six, eight, we ain't gonna integrate!"

Meanwhile, the black students faced their own problems inside the school. The pressure of sneaking into the school and the hostility of the protesters was too much for Thelma. She slumped down on a bench in the school office. She was pale and out of breath, and her lips and fingertips were blue. The rest of the students were told to get to their homerooms.

As Melba walked to her class, a white student came up to her, slapped her in the face, and spit on her. Shaken and confused, Melba could only continue on to class. She would not remain there long, though. She and the other black students would soon have to leave the school.

55

Little Rock police tried to control the mob outside the school, but they were fighting a losing battle.

The local police did not think they could control the mob, and school officials were getting nervous that violence would erupt. They decided the nine black students should leave school for their own safety. The children gathered in the school office while the adults decided how best to get them out of the school. All of the kids were scared, and some of them were crying.

Melba overheard the school officials talking. One man said that the mob had broken through the police barricade and was rushing toward the school. He thought that the kids would be trapped inside. He actually suggested that they turn one of the black students over to the mob so that the others could get out safely. Melba was so afraid that she thought she would collapse. Then she heard another voice say:

> *They're children. What'll we do, have them draw straws to see which one gets a rope around their neck?*

At 11:30 A.M., several police officers took the students out of the principal's office. They led the children quickly down into the basement of the school and put them into cars. As soon as everyone was in, the officers raced out through a back delivery entrance and away from the school.

Police officers made an announcement to the crowd outside that the black students had left the building. But the mob refused to break up until they could send someone inside to make sure the kids really were gone. A white student's mother was allowed inside to make sure the police were telling the truth.

VIOLENT HATRED

After the Little Rock Nine were taken out of school, the angry crowd left the grounds. But some protesters were still looking for trouble—and were willing to take their anger out on any black person unlucky enough to cross their paths. Two women who were driving near the school were pulled from their car and beaten. Two black men were also attacked, and the windows of their truck were smashed.

57

When news of the incident at Central High School reached President Eisenhower, he realized that he had to act. That evening he addressed the country:

> *I will use the full power of the United States, including whatever force may be necessary, to prevent any obstruction of the law and to carry out the orders of the Federal Court.*

President Eisenhower faced off against Governor Faubus to uphold the ruling of the Supreme Court.

Using the full power of the United States, in this case, meant that the president was going to send U.S. Army troops to Little Rock the next day. Later, he federalized the National Guard, which meant that they had to take orders from the U.S. government, not from Governor Faubus of Arkansas. The soldiers who had first kept the black students out of school were now taking orders from the president. This time, they were ordered to protect the Little Rock Nine.

ECHOES OF RECONSTRUCTION

When President Eisenhower sent regular U.S. Army troops into Arkansas, it sent shockwaves through the community. It was the first time since Reconstruction that federal troops were being used to keep the peace in a Southern state. Reconstruction was the period after the Civil War when federal troops occupied the former Confederate states. The presence of U.S. troops in Arkansas brought back a lot of bad memories.

On September 24, the Little Rock Nine again stayed home from school. It was clear that the Little Rock Police Department could not protect them from the angry white crowds. In fact, some police officers had turned in their badges at the school and took the side of the protesters.

That evening, the children gathered at Daisy Bates' house. She told them that they must return to school as soon as it was safe—that they could not give up now. When the president ordered troops into Little Rock, they all saw it as a glimmer of hope that they would be able to attend school without fear of attack. ▰

Screaming Eagles at Central High School

Chapter

6

On September 24, 1957, approximately 1,200 paratroopers from the U.S. Army's famous 101st Airborne Division, which was also known as the Screaming Eagles, landed at the Little Rock Air Force base. The Screaming Eagles immediately took up positions around Little Rock's Central High School.

Daisy Bates began calling the families of the Little Rock Nine at 1 A.M. After weeks of harassing phone calls, however, none of them wanted to answer their phones. Many had even left their phones off the hook. Bates and two principals from black schools then went around to each of the students' homes to tell them about the plan for the next day. They were going back to school to try again, and they were going to go together.

Members of the 101st Airborne Division marched to Central High School to restore order and ensure black students could enter the school.

At 8:30 A.M., the students waited at the Bates house for Army escorts to take them to school. Many of the students' parents were crying, but not out of sadness. Minnijean Brown said what many of them were thinking:

The Little Rock Nine were surrounded by their U.S. Army escorts every time they entered or left the school.

> *For the first time in my life, I feel like an American citizen.*

For as long as they could remember, African-Americans had been treated like second-class citizens. The police did not protect them from racist attacks. In fact, police officers often took part in such activities. Their own government had denied them the most basic human and civil rights for hundreds of years. Now, finally, their country was standing up for them, willing to protect them.

THE BEST OF THE BEST

Formed during World War II, the 101st Airborne Division is made up of troops who are dropped into combat by helicopter or airplane behind enemy lines. Known by the nickname "Screaming Eagles," the 101st Airborne Division has had many successes in combat and is highly respected.

Everyone at the Bates house that day was filled with gratitude and pride. The time had finally come when they could enjoy the same rights that white Americans were able to take for granted.

At 9:22 A.M., the Little Rock Nine entered Central High School. They were surrounded by 20 soldiers. As they entered the building, they saw that soldiers were on duty inside the school as well. Each of the students was assigned a soldier, who escorted him or her from class to class. Although the presence of the armed escorts gave the students a measure of protection, the escorts were only allowed in the hallways. Once the students entered a classroom, restroom, or the lunchroom, they were on their own.

It did not take long for the nine students to realize that they had to be extra careful in order to stay safe. They did not linger in the restrooms, the gym locker rooms, or in isolated areas. They were careful on the staircases. They made sure not to lose sight of their escorts in the crowded hallways between classes.

Not every white student in the school was hostile, of course. Some smiled at the black students and even invited them to share a lunch table. But the segregationists threatened white students as well as black. White students who were friendly to black students ran the risk of being threatened or attacked themselves. It was not long before even the students who were sympathetic toward the Little Rock Nine were too afraid to show any hint of friendliness.

On September 25, something happened that would take away the small sense of security the students had. The *Arkansas Democrat* printed a photo that made it look as if soldiers were marching white girls down the street with bayonets at their backs. Segregationists quickly seized the chance to use the picture to their advantage. It stirred up rage in the South, and Governor Faubus took the opportunity to add fuel to the fire.

On the night of September 26, Governor Faubus appeared on national television and said that his state was an occupied territory. His comment was perfectly designed to make Southerners angry. The federal government reacted quickly, and on October 1, they replaced the soldiers of the 101st with federalized National Guardsmen. President Eisenhower thought that people would find the National Guard easier to accept, since they were from Arkansas. The problem was that these citizen-soldiers did little to protect the Little Rock Nine. ◣

A FEDERAL CASE

Although President Eisenhower was an important figure in the integration of Central High School, he did not really like dealing with racial issues. In fact, he sent federal troops to Arkansas because it was his job to uphold the law as determined by the Supreme Court—not because he supported integration.

School Daze

After the National Guardsmen were ordered to protect the students, it quickly became clear that they were not up to the job. Many of the local men who were in the National Guard were just as set against integration as the most hardcore segregationists. By the end of the first day the National Guardsmen were in the school, most of the 101st was back. But the long-term plan was to reduce the presence of soldiers over time. One way or another, the black students would have to learn how to survive on their own. It would not be easy, though. The segregationists in school were determined to torment the black students any way they could.

Segregationists harassed black students. They would follow a black student around school and step on his or her heels all day until they bled.

Other students would wait by the staircase to push a passing black student down. Other kids simply tripped, punched, or spit on the students as they passed them in the hall. Nasty remarks were made all day, every day. In addition to calling the black students names, the white students would whisper threats as they passed the Little Rock Nine in the hallways. Others would chant the little verse they wrote and handed out to other students: "Two, four, six, eight, we ain't gonna integrate." Segregationists made it their mission to never let the black students forget that they were not wanted in Central High School.

Members of the Screaming Eagles formed a line around the black students as they entered a car to leave school at the end of their first day.

On one occasion, Melba Pattillo was in a bathroom stall when the other girls in the room started throwing flaming paper in on her. Another time, a boy threw acid in her face. Only the quick action of her Army guard saved her from being blinded.

On October 2, a group of about 50 white students chased Jefferson Thomas and Terrence Roberts through the school hallways. When they caught up to them, some boys knocked the books out of the black students' hands. As Jeff and Terry bent down to retrieve their books, they were punched and kicked. The National Guardsmen on duty in the hallway watched the whole thing and did not do anything to help.

Luckily for the boys, Central High School's Assistant Principal Elizabeth Huckaby also saw what happened, and three white boys were suspended for their actions. One of the white boys bragged to the *Arkansas Gazette*:

> *We wanted to make it so miserable, they would not want to go to the school.*

Even though they were afraid to show their support openly, not all white students were vicious toward the black students. Some white students did their best to reach out to the new students. Ernest Green said students would send him private notes that said that they "regret" the situation and told him to keep his chin up.

White students got used to the presence of the National Guard at their school.

A white student also secretly befriended Melba Pattillo. He was friendly with some of the segregationists and so was able to warn Melba about bad things they were planning. In this way, Melba and the other eight students were sometimes able to steer clear of trouble.

Elizabeth Eckford divided the students into three groups for a newspaper reporter:

> *The majority who are civil-minded and courteous and who might like Negroes if they had a chance; those who antagonize verbally and not physically; and those who try to do physical harm to us. I knew it was going to be rough but knowing it and experiencing it are different things.*

69

Each student's Army escort was fully armed and ready for action.

On November 12, Jefferson Thomas was standing next to his locker when he noticed two white boys drawing near. They were pushing and shoving each other, which put Jeff on high alert. A common racist trick was to pretend to be fighting near a black student and then to "accidentally" crash into him or her. This way, if they were caught, they could pretend they were just fooling around. As Jefferson kept an eye on the two boys, another snuck up behind him and knocked him unconscious with a blow to the head. He had to be taken out of school and brought to a doctor. The next day, when Daisy Bates called the Thomas home to check on Jefferson, she was told that he was going to school. He was sure that if the bullies knew they could force him to stay out of school, it would only encourage them.

> ## SCARY BUSINESS
>
> Daisy Bates also experienced violence at her home from the moment she started working on integrating Little Rock's public schools. Someone threw a rock through her window with a note that read: "Next time it will be a bomb." Others burned crosses on her lawn and threw firebombs at her house.

The Little Rock Nine fought back the only way they could: by refusing to be intimidated and refusing to back down. Interestingly, the best way they could fight back was by not taking the segregationists' bait and actually fighting back. They each realized that if they were to get kicked out of school for fighting, it would jeopardize everything they had worked so hard for. Unfortunately, Minnijean was eventually pushed too far.

Even though the black students knew that they would not be allowed to participate in extra-curricular activities, Minnijean was sure that once the white students heard her sing they would want her to perform in the school pageant. Despite the rejection of school officials and the other students, she refused to stop trying. But by December, her upbeat attitude had started to fade.

The Little Rock Nine shared Thanksgiving dinner with Daisy Bates and her husband, L.C.

At lunchtime on December 17, Minnijean struck back at two students who had been taunting her. She dumped a bowl of chili over their heads and was suspended for six days. Minnijean was allowed back into school on January 13 after agreeing that she would never retaliate to any harassment again. But just one month later, Minnijean was expelled after she called a girl who was harassing her "white trash." The segregationists could not have been happier. Some even made up cards that read "One down ... eight to go!" and handed them out in the school.

New Beginnings

After her expulsion, Minnijean was welcomed to New Lincoln High School in New York City. She graduated from that school in 1959. Though her friends were sad to see her go, Minnijean was relieved. "I'll be so glad when I am just an ordinary student," she said.

The card-bearers would never get their wish, though. It was more than difficult, but the remaining eight black students made it through the rest of the school year. In the spring of 1958, Ernest Green became the first African-American to graduate from Central High School. Four thousand people were on hand as he crossed the stage on graduation day. But no one except his family and their guest, the Reverend Martin Luther King Jr., applauded as Ernie received his diploma.

Melba listened to Ernie's graduation on the radio with her family and felt bad when the audience did not applaud her friend. Melba's mother comforted her daughter by saying:

Ernest Green was the first of the Little Rock Nine to graduate.

> *Lots of people in the rest of the world are applauding for Ernie and for all of you who made it through this year.*

Melba's grandmother had a different response. She said:

> *Who cares if they applaud. At least they didn't shoot him.*

Even though Ernest and his friends had accomplished their goal and attended Central High School, Governor Faubus kept trying to stop integration. Following Ernest's graduation, segregationists in Arkansas got ready to prevent the seven remaining black students from following in his shoes.

Once again, the Little Rock School Board asked for an injunction delaying integration until 1961. This time was different, though. They were trying to avoid trouble rather than simply avoiding integration. They knew that Governor Faubus would be out of office by 1961, so he would be powerless to stir up more trouble over integration.

The Supreme Court eventually denied the school board's request to delay integration. But Governor Faubus was determined to make sure that integration was stopped one way or another. After the Supreme Court's decision to move forward with integration, the governor simply shut down all the public schools across Arkansas.

75

The 1958–1959 school year brought back memories from the year before, when the Little Rock Nine, including Minnijean, Melba, and Thelma, worked together at home to keep up on their studies.

During the 1958–1959 school year, the seven black students—along with everyone else—waited to hear when they could return to school. Meanwhile, their families and others in their community were under incredible pressure. Some people lost their jobs or were forced to resign because they would not convince the black students to give up on integration. Terrence Roberts' family moved to Los Angeles, California, where he finished high school. Gloria Ray's and Elizabeth Eckford's families also moved away.

Summer Fun

In the summer of 1958, the Little Rock Nine got the chance to leave all the bad experiences of the school year behind them. Together with Daisy Bales, they toured the United States where, in the North, they were treated like heroes. The children were given many awards during their travels, including the Spingarn Medal, which is awarded every year by the NAACP for outstanding achievement by a black American. Other famous people who have received the medal include Jackie Robinson, Martin Luther King Jr., Rosa Parks, Oprah Winfrey, and Colin Powell.

Meanwhile, the remaining four students took correspondence courses from the University of Arkansas while they waited for the public schools to re-open. Jefferson and Carlotta both completed their junior year this way. Thelma and Melba, who both should have been enjoying their senior year in high school in 1958–1959, received their diplomas in the mail. ◣

Looking Back

In the summer of 1959, the law that Governor Faubus had used to shut down Little Rock's public schools was declared unconstitutional. The governor quickly got to work drafting a new law that would allow him to keep the schools closed. But the Little Rock School Board beat him to the punch. The city's high schools were opened early, on August 12, before the governor had a chance to act. Jefferson Thomas and Carlotta Walls returned to Central High School and graduated that spring.

Another integrated high school in Little Rock, Hall High, was opened that year as well. Three black students were sent there. Both Jefferson and Carlotta, however, felt that it was important they return to Central.

Jefferson later said:

> *It became even more important to graduate because I guess I had to prove something to myself that I wouldn't cave or give in under stress or adversity, that I was as tough as, you know, any teenager ... I can take anything you can dish out and as long as I can take it, I'm better than you are.*

Members of the Little Rock Nine posed on the steps of the U.S. Supreme Court with Daisy Bates and attorney Thurgood Marshall.

The students had their picture taken with Mayor Robert Wagner in New York City.

According to Carlotta, it was the values she learned at home that made her able to rise above the hatred and adversity she faced every day at school. The moral strength and support of her family were what enabled her to reach her goal of receiving a diploma from Central High School. In later years, Carlotta recalled how she coped with the challenges of integrating an all-white school in the South:

> *I was not taught to hate. I didn't hate anyone. I considered them ignorant. I was above all of that stuff. The name-calling and the harassment, I had to be mentally above that. It was more like a job for me. I got up and went to work every day. That's what it became. When it was over, my job was done. When I received that diploma, my commitment was over. I was determined to get that because they didn't want me to have it.*

After graduating, each of the Little Rock Nine went on to college, thanks partly to scholarship money that Daisy Bates raised through the NAACP. Later, Ernest served as the Assistant Secretary of Labor under President Jimmy Carter, and after that, he became a financial consultant. Minnijean lived on a farm in Canada with her husband and six children, but later returned to Little Rock. Thelma Mothershed was a school teacher in Illinois for 28 years.

Elizabeth returned to Little Rock to raise her family, where she was a substitute teacher before becoming a probation officer. Melba became a TV reporter and writer. Gloria became a computer science writer and moved to Sweden, her husband's country. Terrence earned his doctorate and became a professor of psychology. Jefferson served in the U.S. Army and later ran a record shop in Los Angeles. Carlotta moved to Denver, Colorado, where she became a real estate agent.

Though her health suffered over the years, Daisy Bates continued to work for civil rights until her death in 1997. She continued to publish her newspaper, the *Arkansas State Press*, which had always been vocal about issues of racial equality, for many years. She wrote an autobiography called *The Long Shadow of Little Rock* and even spoke at the famous March on Washington in 1963—one of the defining events of the civil rights movement. Daisy always argued for fair treatment of African-Americans, even after a stroke took her ability to speak. Even though she needed a wheelchair for mobility at that point, she carried the Olympic torch in the 1996 Atlanta games.

The crisis in Little Rock had an incredible effect on the rest of the country—and the rest of the world. It showed just how far certain Southerners were willing to go to stop integration. It showed very clearly how dangerous it was to be black in certain parts of America. But more importantly, it showed African-Americans that they could effect change—that they could attain the rights they deserved. The impact of the Little Rock integration was summed up in later years by Daisy Bates, who said:

> *The lunch counter sit-ins, the Freedom Rides, and similar struggles in which Negroes, led by Negroes, successfully engaged in after Little Rock would possibly have taken place at some time in the future in any case. But that these events occurred when they did is*

probably due more to the impact of Little Rock than to any other factor. ... Events in history occur when the time has ripened for them, but they need a spark. Little Rock was that spark at that stage of the struggle of the American Negro for justice.

In 1996, Daisy Bates carried the Olympic torch during the celebration of the summer games in Atlanta, Georgia.

Olym   n Re

As time passed, the sacrifices made by the Little Rock Nine were recognized and celebrated on a national level. In 1997, on the 40th anniversary of the Little Rock integration, the nine students gathered in their hometown for a celebration with President Bill Clinton. During his speech, the president talked about just how much the Little Rock Nine had done for the country:

> *I want all these children here to look at these people. They persevered. They endured. And they prevailed. But it was at great cost to themselves. ... Like so many Americans, I*

U.S. President Bill Clinton spoke at a memorial service for Daisy Bates in 1997.

> *can never fully repay my debt to these*
> *nine people. For, with their innocence, they*
> *purchased more freedom for me, too, and for*
> *all white people.*

The next year, on November 6, 1998, Central High School was designated a National Historic Site. In 1999, the Little Rock Nine were awarded the Congressional Medal of Honor for their actions in 1957–1958. The Congressional Medal of Honor is the nation's highest civilian honor. And in 2005, a monument to the nine was unveiled in front of the Arkansas governor's office. The bronze statues show Ernest, Minnijean, Terrence, Elizabeth, Thelma, Gloria, Melba, Jefferson, and Carlotta walking together with their books in their hands, as they did in 1957 entering Little Rock Central High School.

When reading about the integration of Central High School, it is easy to forget that the warriors on the frontlines of this battle were just children. But as often happened during the civil rights movement, these ordinary people found the strength to do extraordinary things. By showing up at Central High School day after day and holding their heads high despite the abuse, the Little Rock Nine changed the world for the better. Their struggle and sacrifice made it possible for all people to enjoy the rights and opportunities that should be available to everyone. Just as important, their actions served as an example and inspiration to others who wanted to make a difference. ◣

Timeline

1849

The Massachusetts Supreme Court rules that segregated schools are allowed under the state's constitution. This ruling will later be used by the U.S. Supreme Court to support the concept of "separate but equal."

1899

The U.S. Supreme Court rules that a state can tax black and white citizens while only providing a public school for white children.

May 17, 1954

Segregation in public schools is declared unconstitutional in *Brown v. Board of Education.*

May 22, 1954

The Little Rock School Board says it will abide by the Supreme Court's decision as soon as it receives details on how and when to proceed with integration.

1955

The Supreme Court orders integration to proceed "with all deliberate speed" in its *Brown* ruling.

May 24, 1955

The Little Rock School Board votes to adopt the Blossom Plan.

1956

Ten thousand young people march in Washington, D.C., in support of integration.

January 23, 1956

Thirty-three students attempt to register in all-white Little Rock schools, but are turned down.

February 8, 1956

The NAACP files a suit on behalf of the 33 black students, claiming discrimination.

August 28, 1956

The NAACP suit is dismissed; lawyers file an appeal.

1957

The Little Rock School Board is ordered to begin the integration of Central High School in September.

Summer 1957

People opposed to integration organize the Capital Citizens Council and the Mothers' League of Central High School.

August 27, 1957

Mrs. Clyde A. Thomason, a member of the Mothers' League, goes to court for a temporary injunction against school integration. It is granted.

August 30, 1957

Federal District Judge Ronald Davies nullifies the injunction.

September 2, 1957

Governor Faubus calls out the National Guard to prevent integration of Central High School.

September 3, 1957

None of the Little Rock Nine attends the first official day of school.

September 4, 1957

National Guardsmen bar the Little Rock Nine from entering Central High School.

September 20, 1957

President Eisenhower orders Governor Faubus to remove National Guard troops from the school.

September 23, 1957

The Little Rock Nine enter Central High School through a side entrance but are removed for their own protection within a few hours.

September 24, 1957

Little Rock Mayor Woodrow Mann sends President Eisenhower a telegram asking for help and troops. The president sends the 101st Airborne Division and federalizes the National Guard.

September 25, 1957

The Little Rock Nine attend their first full day of classes at Central High School under the protection of their 101st Airborne guards.

1958

The Supreme Court rules that fear of violence doesn't excuse state governments from following the *Brown v. Board of Education* ruling.

February 1958

Minnijean Brown is expelled for fighting back against her tormentors.

May 1958

Ernest Brown becomes the first African-American to graduate from Central High School.

1958–1959

Little Rock public schools are closed for the year by order of Governor Faubus.

Timeline

1959

Twenty-five thousand young people march in Washington, D.C., in support of integration.

May 1959

Closing of the Little Rock public schools is declared unconstitutional.

August 12, 1959

Little Rock schools start the school year; integration continues.

1960

Federal marshals are sent to protect 6-year-old Ruby Bridges from an angry mob as she attempts to enroll in school in New Orleans.

1962

The University of Mississippi is ordered to admit James Meredith, an African-American student. More than 2,000 white people riot on the day Meredith arrives at school.

1963

For the first time, black students attend public schools in Alabama, Louisiana, and Mississippi with white students.

1968

The Supreme Court orders states to completely take apart their segregated school systems "root and branch."

1969

The Supreme Court rules that "all deliberate speed" is no longer permissible. All Mississippi schools are ordered to desegregate immediately.

Fall 1972

All grade levels in the Little Rock public school system are finally integrated.

October 24, 1987

Thirty years after integrating Central High School, the Little Rock Nine return to the school as a group for the first time to celebrate with Lottie Shackelford, Little Rock's second black mayor, and Central students.

1988

With almost 45 percent of black students in the United States attending majority-white schools, integration reaches an all-time high.

September 1997

The Little Rock Nine gather together with President Bill Clinton to celebrate the 40th anniversary of Central High School's integration.

November 9, 1999

The Little Rock Nine are presented with the Congressional Medal of Honor.

On the Web

For more information on *The Little Rock Nine*, use FactHound.

1 Go to *www.facthound.com*

2 Type in this book ID: 0756520118

3 Click on the *Fetch It* button. FactHound will find Web sites related to this book.

Historic Sites

Central High School National Historic Site
2124 Daisy L. Gatson Bates Drive
Little Rock, AR 72202

The site of the Little Rock Nine's struggle against segregation is still a working high school.

Arkansas State Capitol
Little Rock, AR 72201

Visitors can view "Testament," the group of sculptures created to honor the achievements of the Little Rock Nine, at the Arkansas State Capitol building.

Look For More Books in This Series

The Collapse of the Soviet Union:
The End of an Empire
ISBN 0-7565-2009-6

Hurricane Katrina
Aftermath of Disaster
ISBN 0-7565-2101-7

McCarthyism:
The Red Scare
ISBN 0-7565-2007-X

Miranda v. Arizona:
The Rights of the Accused
ISBN 0-7565-2008-8

The New Deal:
Rebuilding America
ISBN 0-7565-2096-7

Watergate:
Scandal in the White House
ISBN 0-7565-2010-X

A complete list of **Snapshots in History** titles is available on our Web site: *www.compasspointbooks.com*

Glossary

abolish
to put an end to something

activist
someone who takes part in supporting a cause

adversity
hardship or misfortune

assurance
promise, guarantee

bigot
a person who treats people of another race with hatred

boycott
to refuse to do business with someone as a sign of protest

committed
dedicated

consequences
the effects of a person's actions.

discriminate
to treat a group of people unfairly, usually because of race

implement
put into practice

injunction
a court order that stops someone from following through on an action

integrate
to make something available to all races

isolated
all alone

jeer
taunt, make fun of

jeopardize
put at risk

landmark
a decisive moment

negotiate
try to come to an agreement

penalized
punished

petition
a serious plea or request to a person or persons in authority

racism
the belief that one race is better than others

retaliate
strike back

segregation
the separation of a group of people from the rest of society based on race

Source Notes

Chapter 1

Page 10, lines 14, 19: Daisy Bates. *The Long Shadow of Little Rock: A Memoir.*
Fayetteville: University of Arkansas Press, 1987, p. 74.

Page 11, line 13: Ibid., p. 75.

Page 13, lines 4, 9: Ibid.

Page 13, lines 13, 19: "Making a Crisis in Arkansas." *Time*
16 Sept. 1957, p. 75.

Page 14, line 19: *The Long Shadow of Little Rock: A Memoir,* p. 76.

Chapter 2

Page 25, sidebar: Judith Bloom Fradin and Dennis Brindell Fradin.
The Power of One: Daisy Bates and the Little Rock Nine. New York:
Clarion Books, 2004, pp. 32–33.

Page 29, line 24: Ibid., p. 74.

Page 30, sidebar: "7 Kids Who Tried." *New York Post* 1 Nov. 1957.

Chapter 3

Page 34, line 22: *The Power of One: Daisy Bates and the Little Rock Nine,* p. 65.

Page 36, line 24: U.S. Dept. of State. "Little Rock Nine Speak About 1957
Integration Struggle." June 2005. 31 Jan. 2006. http://usinfo.state.gov/scv/
Archive/2005/Jun/30-644847.html

Page 38, line 17: *The Power of One: Daisy Bates and the Little Rock Nine,* p. 67.

Page 39, line 2: Melba Pattillo Beals. *Warriors Don't Cry.* New York:
Washington Square Press, 1994, p. 28.

Page 40, line 21: Ibid., p. 36.

Chapter 4

Page 47, line 2: Ibid., p. 55.

Page 48, line 11: "Week of Drama." *New York Times* 8 Sept. 1957.

Page 49, line 17: "Nine Negroes Marking Time Until CHS Dispute
Settled." *Arkansas Gazette* 16 Sept. 1957.

Source Notes

Chapter 5

Page 54, line 8: I. Wilmer Counts. *A Life is More Than a Moment: The Desegregation of Little Rock's Central High*. Bloomington: Indiana University Press, 1999, p. 54.

Page 57, line 10: *Warriors Don't Cry*, p. 116.

Page 58, line 5: "September 24 Becomes Ike's Day for Crises." *Arkansas Democrat* 24 Sept. 1957.

Chapter 6

Page 62, line 6: *The Power of One: Daisy Bates and the Little Rock Nine*, p. 95.

Chapter 7

Page 68, line 21: *The Power of One: Daisy Bates and the Little Rock Nine*, p. 108.

Page 69, line 9: "Little Rock: More Tension Than Ever." *New York Times* 23 Mar. 1958.

Page 73, sidebar: "School Welcomes Little Rock Girl." *New York Times* 25 Feb. 1958.

Page 75, lines 1, 6: *Warriors Don't Cry*, p. 304.

Chapter 8

Page 79, line 2: "Opening Doors and Minds." *PBS Online Newshour*. 25 Sept. 1997. 27 April 2006. www.pbs.org/newshour/bb/race_relations/july-dec97/rock_9-25.html

Page 81, line 3: "A Higher Moral Power." *The Madison Times* 20 May 2005.

Page 82, line 26: "Public Schools Shut Down" 31 Jan. 2006. 27 April 2006. www.watson.org/~lisa/blackhistory/school-integration/lilrock/shutdown.html

Page 84, line 9: "Clinton Honors Little Rock Nine." *CNN.com*. 2006. 25 Sept. 1997. www.cnn.com/US/9709/26/little.rock.anniv/

Select Bibliography

Bates, Daisy. *The Long Shadow of Little Rock: A Memoir.* Fayetteville: University of Arkansas Press, 1987.

Beals, Melba Pattillo. *Warriors Don't Cry.* New York: Washington Square Press, 1994.

Counts, I. Wilmer. *A Life Is More Than a Moment: The Desegregation of Little Rock's Central High.* Bloomington: Indiana University Press, 1999.

Fradin, Judith Bloom, and Dennis Brindell Fradin. *The Power of One: Daisy Bates and the Little Rock Nine.* New York: Clarion Books, 2004.

Huckaby, Elizabeth. *Crisis at Central High, 1957–58.* Baton Rouge: Louisiana State Press, 1980.

Further Reading

Altman, Linda Jacobs. *The American Civil Rights Movement: The African-American Struggle for Equality.* Berkeley Heights, N.J.: Enslow Publishers, 2004.

Finlayson, Reggie. *We Shall Overcome: The History of the American Civil Rights Movement.* Minneapolis: Lerner Publications, 2003.

Fradin, Judith Bloom, and Dennis Brindell Fradin. *The Power of One: Daisy Bates and the Little Rock Nine.* New York: Clarion Books, 2004.

Lucas, Eileen. *Cracking the Wall: The Struggles of the Little Rock Nine.* Minneapolis: Carolrhoda Books, 1997.

Price, Sean. *When Will I Get In? Segregation and Civil Rights.* Chicago: Raintree, 2007.

Index